T0393365

ARETHA FRANKLIN

The Queen of Soul

Celebrating

BLACK ARTISTS

ARETHA
FRANKLIN
The Queen of Soul

Enslow Publishing
101 W. 23rd Street
Suite 240
New York, NY 10011
USA

enslow.com

CHARLOTTE ETINDE-CROMPTON AND
SAMUEL WILLARD CROMPTON

Published in 2020 by Enslow Publishing, LLC.
101 W. 23rd Street, Suite 240, New York, NY 10011

Library of Congress Cataloging-in-Publication Data

Names: Crompton, Samuel Willard, author. | Etinde-Crompton, Charlotte,
author.
Title: Aretha Franklin : the queen of soul / Samuel Willard Crompton and
Charlotte Etinde-Crompton.
Description: New York : Enslow Publishing, 2020. | Series: Celebrating black
artists | Includes bibliographical references and index. | Audience: Grades
7–12.
Identifiers: LCCN 2018015696| ISBN 9781978503571 (library bound) |
ISBN 9781978505322 (pbk.)
Subjects: LCSH: Franklin, Aretha—Juvenile literature. | Soul musicians—
United States—Biography. | African American singers—Biography—Juvenile
literature. | Singers—United States—Biography—Juvenile literature.
Classification: LCC ML3930.F68 C76 2019 | DDC 782.421644092 [B]—dc23
LC record available at https://lccn.loc.gov/2018015696

Printed in China

To Our Readers: We have done our best to make sure all website addresses in
this book were active and appropriate when we went to press. However, the author
and the publisher have no control over and assume no liability for the material
available on those websites or on any websites they may link to. Any comments or
suggestions can be sent by e-mail to customerservice@enslow.com.

Contents

It became clear from a very early age that Aretha Franklin had an astounding talent.

Chapter **1**

Earning R-E-S-P-E-C-T

Born in Memphis, Tennessee, in 1942, Aretha Franklin recorded her eleventh studio album by the time she was twenty-five years old. The reason behind her significant head start is that she learned music in the family home, practically at the feet of her renowned father, C. L. Franklin, who was a legendary figure in both ministry and civil rights activism in the 1950s and 1960s. Singing professionally at the age of fourteen, Aretha Franklin had come a long way as a gospel singer, but she was about to burst into a new genre.

Blessed with a powerful voice, Franklin was already well known to a core constituency—listeners of gospel music. But she was little known to the wider audience of popular music lovers. Franklin changed her recording label from Columbia to Atlantic in 1966 and released the album *I Never Loved a Man the Way I Love You* in the early spring of 1967. The world of popular music was never the same again.

The Breakthrough Album

I Never Loved a Man the Way I Love You contains eleven songs. For attentive listeners of 1967, it was clear that the entire album was a major success. But for casual listeners, one song in particular stood out: "Respect." Originally written and recorded by soul music superstar Otis Redding, this new version of the song struck a chord with fans, establishing Aretha Franklin as a force to be reckoned with. In the original incarnation, Redding sings "All I'm askin' for/ Is a little respect/ When I come home," playing the role of the harried husband, demanding respect in his role as the family breadwinner.

On first hearing the reworked lines on Franklin's album, one imagines an African American housewife or girlfriend, pining for the man in her life. But the more one listens, the bigger the story becomes. Franklin's cover version turned the gender politics on its head and transformed Redding's wearied male complaint into a feminist anthem.[1] Spelling out "respect" in the now iconic chorus of R-E-S-P-E-C-T, Franklin gave the song a brand-new hook, one that was totally irresistible to listeners.

And when "Respect" ruled the airwaves in the summer of 1967, tens of millions of people—black and white, rich and poor, blue collar and white collar—listened with appreciation and excitement. *Rolling Stone* describes it thus:

> Aretha's voice reached out and took hold of you in whatever way you needed it. A radio playing "Respect" could be tuned in at four different households, and each person singing along with "sock-it-to-me" would hear Aretha's phrasings as personal: the working woman, tired of hassle from

Legendary singer Otis Redding originally recorded "Respect," but Aretha Franklin turned the song into a hit.

Otis Redding

Much like Aretha Franklin, Otis Redding began his musical career at a very young age. When he was fifteen years old, Redding dropped out of high school and eventually joined the backing band for rock'n'roll icon Little Richard. In 1964, Redding released his debut album, *Pain in My Heart,* meeting with great success as the album peaked at number twenty on the R&B charts. Redding's songs often contained a powerful feeling of yearning–"These Arms of Mine," "Mr. Pitiful," and "I've Been Loving You Too Long" all convey a sense of longing and loneliness supported by the intensity and passion in Redding's vocals.

Sadly, his promising career was cut short when Redding was just twenty-six years old. On December 10, 1967, Redding and his band boarded a plane in the middle of a severe rainstorm, headed to a performance in Wisconsin. Just 4 miles (6.4 kilometers) away from their destination, the plane crashed, killing almost everyone onboard, including Otis Redding. Perhaps his most famous song, "(Sittin' On) The Dock of the Bay" was released after his death in January 1968. It's the only Redding single to reach number one on the Billboard Hot 100 chart.

the boss; the lover wishing for more from a hesitant mate; the black-and-proud activist, readying himself for another rally; the bouffanted teenager, sick of her parents telling her what to do.[2]

Within a year's time, *I Never Loved a Man the Way I Love You* was purchased 1.2 million times. And five of the singles hit gold, meaning each sold more than one million copies.

True, there had been massive breakthroughs before: One thinks of the Beatles in 1964 and the Rolling Stones in 1966. But those were groups, with as many as four potential voices. In this case, the success was built on one voice, and it happened to belong to a young black American woman. *That* had never happened before.

The Critical Response

Almost every segment of American society registered approval of *I Never Loved a Man the Way I Love You*. It took the critics a little longer to catch up.

Slightly over a year after *I Never Loved A Man the Way I Love You* was released, *Time* magazine weighed in. During this period, *Time* was the most influential of all American periodicals, read by millions. For its June 28, 1968, issue, it put Aretha Franklin on the cover and asked a question:

Has it got soul? Man, that's the question of the hour. If it has soul, then it's tough, beautiful, out of sight. It has the authenticity of collard greens boiling on the stove, the sassy style of the boogaloo in a hip discothèque, the solidarity signified by "Soul Brother" scrawled on a ghetto storefront. But what is soul?[3]

In the early years of her career, Franklin traveled often for performances, taking few breaks.

The question was well-phrased. The answer, on the other hand, was almost impossibly labored. The *Time* magazine writer wrestled with his own question for almost six pages and never quite answered it. Soul, it turned out, was *very* difficult to define. But *Time* did get one important thing right: one knows soul when one hears it. And this was especially true when Aretha Franklin held the microphone.

Even before the *Time* issue was printed, Franklin performed to a sold-out crowd at the Philharmonic Hall in Manhattan, New York. No previous rhythm-and-blues singer had accomplished this feat. *Time* described Franklin's performance: "She leans her head back, forehead gleaming with perspiration, features twisted by her intensity, and her voice—plangent and supple—pierces the hall."[4]

The *Time* article put Aretha Franklin front and center, but a series of photographs, along the side of the page, featured Billie Holliday, B. B. King, Mahalia Jackson, and Janis Joplin. All four of these luminaries knew enormous success; all of them paid a heavy price for their fame. Franklin, too, would be called upon to make sacrifices.

Born to a musical family, Franklin grew up in an environment where the word of God and the lyrics on a sheet of newsprint worked together seamlessly. Raised in Detroit, Michigan, she was the daughter of an enormously talented and influential Baptist minister who had recorded seventy albums of his sermons. But Aretha Franklin's success did not come without a price:

> Driving eight or ten hours trying to make a gig, and being hungry and passing restaurants all along the road, and having to go off the highway into

some little city to find a place to eat because you're black that had its effect.[5]

So did the wear and tear of singing. Franklin cheerfully admitted she was only twenty-six, but she complained that some days she felt like twenty-six going on sixty-five.

Did Aretha Franklin have soul? Would she be able to bring that soul to multigenerational and multiracial audiences? The verdict had already been rendered: a resounding "yes."

Daughter of a Preacher Man

Any biography of Aretha Franklin, short or long, needs to start in the same place and with the same person. The place is the Mississippi Delta, and the person is C. L. Franklin.

Roots in the Deep South

Clarence LaVaughn Franklin, whom everyone referred to as "C. L.," was born in Sunflower County, Mississippi, in January 1915. He was the son of sharecroppers—African American farmers who worked the land as tenants—hoping against hope to get ahead. But unfortunately for sharecroppers, nine times out of ten they fell behind.

While it's widely acknowledged that life in the South has been especially difficult for black Americans, the Mississippi Delta was one of the worst, most inhospitable places in the Deep South. The area was infamous for the number of lynchings and the specific brutality with which they were

Admired by many and distrusted by others, C.L. Franklin was an outstanding minister, whose sermons paved the way for his daughter's early success in gospel.

carried out. The First World War provided a brief respite. Thousands of young black men left the Delta to serve in the US Army, and many came back with improved ideas of their self-worth. These ideas did not endear them to the white population, and the lynchings grew apace.

Young C. L. Franklin was aware of the dangers of being a black young man in an area so rife with racism. He had only a slight familiarity with the changes brought by World War I; his father abandoned the family shortly after returning from service in France. Franklin's mother soon remarried, and C. L. took his stepfather's name.

Almost everything seemed rigged against this boy of the Mississippi Delta. He seemed doomed to remain in poverty for life. But no matter how hard or painful the obstacles were, C. L. Franklin was not convinced that the situation

Mississippi Blues

Blues is a genre of music that developed around the turn of the twentieth century. Drawing on black spirituals and African traditional music, the emergence of the blues is closely tied to the end of slavery and the beginning of free black expression in America. While no one place, or even state, can claim to be the original starting point of the blues, the Mississippi Delta comes closer than most. Numerous leading musicians, including B. B. King and Fats Waller, hailed from the Delta.

was hopeless. He sincerely believed that he would rise in the world.

The Pasture Pastor

At nine or ten years of age, C. L. Franklin had a powerful religious experience at St. Peter's Baptist Church. Like many other African American boys, he answered an "altar call," going forward to deliver testimony. Unlike many of his contemporaries, C. L. Franklin felt "called" for life.

In the middle of outdoors work, he would stop plowing and preach spontaneously, with nothing more than a horse or mule for company. The teenage boy became known as the "pasture pastor." His impromptu sermons were impressive: C. L. had a fine tenor voice, which became better with the passage of years.

At the age of sixteen, C. L. asked his parents to allow him to travel and preach. Leaving home for the first time, he set out on a two-year journey, right in the middle of the Great Depression. C. L. Franklin worked temporary jobs, preached when he could, and gained a first-rate education in the "school of hard knocks." By the time he came home, at eighteen, he was a man and ready to commence his life career.

C. L.'s mother and stepfather gave their blessing, and he departed. The following year found him in Shelby, Mississippi, and the year after that he was in Memphis, Tennessee. Wherever he went, C. L. impressed people with his energy and style. He was unrefined, but there was great potential beneath the rough surface. Many people noticed the young man and commented on how he would go places. One person who took him especially seriously was Barbara L. Siggers.

Lighter-skinned and more financially secure than C. L., Barbara Siggers was several rungs above him on the African American social ladder. Her friends and family cautioned her that C. L. came from the wrong side of the tracks, but she was won over by his earnest courtship and obvious potential. The couple married in 1938. At about the same time, C. L. gained his first full-time pastorate in Memphis.

Start of a Family

After C. L. Franklin adopted Barbara's son, Vaughn, he and Barbara proceeded to have four other children, for a

The Secret of a Son

For many years, the Franklins took pride in raising all five of their children: Erma, Cecil, Aretha, Carolyn, and their eldest, Vaughn. But there was a long concealed family secret: Vaughn was not actually C. L. Franklin's son. In 1934, prior to meeting and marrying Franklin, Barbara had another romantic relationship that resulted in Vaughn's birth. Nonetheless, Franklin formally and secretly adopted the boy soon after he married Barbara in 1938. It wasn't until 1951, several years after Barbara and C. L. Franklin ended their relationship for good, that Vaughn Franklin discovered the truth.

Preservationists are working to restore Aretha Franklin's childhood home in Memphis, Tennessee.

total of five in the family. Aretha Franklin, fourth of the five in birth order, was born in Memphis on March 25, 1942: "Three months after the attack on Pearl Harbor, while the world was ablaze in war, I made my debut. I was born Aretha Louise Franklin on March 25, 1942, named after my father's two sisters, Aretha and Louise."[1] The opening words of Aretha Franklin's autobiography do not seem especially revealing: many Americans could claim similar circumstances. But the way Franklin joined her fate and concerns with those of the nation remained a lasting part of her personality. For decades to come, she would link her own life to social, cultural, and even national events.

Aretha Franklin was not yet two when the family moved to Buffalo, New York. Naturally, she had few, if any, memories of Memphis, and even when she visited in later years, she felt and displayed little connection to the area. The home in which she was born is a small double-frame construction. It attracts thousands of sightseers and music fans.

A Northern Cold

The move from Memphis to Buffalo was as significant as one might imagine. C. L. Franklin later poked fun at the change in climate, saying it did more good than harm, but Buffalo was—and is—one of the coldest of American cities. And as it turned out, the Franklins did not stay there long.

By the time Aretha Franklin turned four years old, the Franklin family had picked up and moved to Detroit's East Side. C. L. Franklin delivered a stirring address at a Detroit event, and he was invited to assume leadership of the New Salem Baptist Church. Aretha Franklin retained some memories of Buffalo, but her worldview was shaped by the early years in Detroit.

Her personality was also shaped by a major trauma, the fact of which she consistently denied. Here she describes it in her autobiography:

> My parents separated when I was six. Despite the fact that it has been written innumerable times, it is an absolute lie that my mother abandoned us. In no way, shape, form, or fashion did our mother desert us….She simply moved with Vaughn back to Buffalo, where she lived with her parents.[2]

While an outside observer might be tempted to judge Barbara Franklin harshly for her decision to leave, it is highly likely that C. L. Franklin's hectic schedule and infidelity contributed to the demise of their marriage and Barbara's departure from the family. There were rumors of multiple affairs, but undoubtedly the most shocking liaison was his relationship with twelve-year-old Mildred Jennings, which resulted in a son, Carl Ellan Kelley. While Mildred was ostracized from the community for her part in the affair, Franklin continued to preach; he didn't acknowledge Carl Ellan as his son until 1958.[3]

In 1940, divorce was frowned upon, leaving Barbara with few options but to stay with her husband. It wasn't until 1948 that Barbara would leave C. L. and move back to Buffalo. The children would spend summers with Barbara in Buffalo, and she would visit them in Detroit while they attended school and lived with their father for much of the year.[4] Though she would go on to bond with and rely on her father, Aretha Franklin clearly never held her mother responsible for this painful separation.

Daddy's Girl

Barbara Siggers Franklin and Vaughn Franklin's departure for Buffalo left the remaining four Franklin children effectively without a mother. The children did see their mother during the summer months, but C. L. Franklin's presence and authority filled the space.

Many people have commented on the openness of Reverend C. L. Franklin's Detroit home. It was a warm and cozy place, they declared, one where various kinds of people, nearly all of whom were musically talented, were welcome. There is much truth to the assertion, but it is far from being the whole truth. The Franklin home was not warm and cozy for the Franklin children.

Years later, in her cowritten memoir, Aretha Franklin dwelled on the positive aspects of her upbringing. The pain was mostly concealed. She wrote of the many singers and songwriters who spent time at the Franklin home but did not acknowledge the lack of feminine leadership. With Aretha's mother gone, C. L. had the run of things.

While Barbara Siggers Franklin and her son Vaughn returned to Buffalo, the rest of the Franklin family stayed in Detroit, pictured here.

A Sudden Loss

Years later, Aretha Franklin recalled the painful events of 1952, one of the most terrible moments of her life:

> Daddy called all of us—me, Erma, Carolyn, and Cecil—into the kitchen. As he sat at the end of the sink, which resembled a sideboard, he said it plainly and solemnly. Our mother had suffered a fatal heart attack. I just stood there, stunned. I cannot describe the pain, nor will I try. Pain is sometimes a private matter.[1]

Barbara Siggers Franklin was only thirty-four. To say this was a serious tragedy is an understatement. The Franklin children were all devastated. But the emotional effect seemed strongest on Aretha, who was just ten years old. She withdrew into herself, at the same time that new demands were placed on her. These came primarily from her father.

The Rise of C. L. Franklin

C. L. Franklin had always been ambitious, so much that family and neighbors back home in the Mississippi Delta

Aretha Franklin often performed at the New Bethel Baptist Church in Detroit, where her father was the pastor.

marveled at his gumption. Becoming pastor of the New Bethel Baptist Church in Detroit was a major balm to Franklin's ambition, but he pushed for more. At about the same time his wife died, C. L. began having recordings of his sermons made. At first he had them produced locally, for his congregation, but before long they were being recorded and distributed by Chess Records.

C. L.'s voice was as powerful as his ambition. Using the punctuations of "whoo" and "ahh" he had learned in the Mississippi Delta, he brought this style to his Detroit congregation and then beyond. No less a figure than the Reverend Jesse Jackson later asserted that virtually all African American preachers attempted either to imitate C. L. Franklin or cast themselves as his exact opposite. In either case, his example could not be avoided.

Her Father's Attention

While C. L. continued to rise to prominence, Aretha Franklin was on the hunt for a substitute mother. For years, she believed, and fervently hoped, that her father would marry the well-known African American singer Clara Ward. This hope may have persuaded Aretha to do her best in music, as a way of bringing her father and her hoped-for mother together. But the talent that propelled Aretha existed even before her mother's death:

> On some nights after I had gone to bed, out of the darkness I'd hear a knock on the door and Daddy saying, "Ree, come on downstairs. I'd like you to play and sing a couple of things"...I was sleepy and didn't want to drag myself out of bed. But I was an obedient daughter and did what Daddy

asked...I slid onto the piano bench and played Canadian Sunset.[2]

At this early stage, Aretha's vocal potential was not the star attraction. Rather, it was her skill on the piano that drew attention. She did not learn to read music by sight; instead, she listened, imitated, and improvised. She got better all the time.

First Performances

The date on which Aretha Franklin first performed at New Bethel Baptist Church has not been preserved. What we do know, beyond the shadow of a doubt, is that this performance was highly successful. The twelve-year-old Aretha made a splash that first time, and she soon became a regular member of the New Bethel choir.

C. L. Franklin swiftly took his talented daughter on the road. By 1955, C.L. had a regular traveling gospel group. One of the earliest descriptions of a C. L. Franklin gospel concert comes from a Virginia newspaper, in 1957:

> A capacity audience was present at the Norfolk Municipal Auditorium on Sunday afternoon, March 24, to hear the noted evangelist, Reverend C.L. Franklin deliver the principal message and be the feature in a mammoth gospel presentation... He also told the Guide that he planned to continue in evangelistic work despite requests being made for him to seek the presidency of a national Baptist convention...Rev. Mr. Franklin's teenage daughter, Miss Aretha Franklin, was also accorded a great ovation for her presentation of "Draw Me Closer."[3]

Learning by Ear

Aretha Franklin fit into a long tradition in the African American musical community. Many black singers learned by ear, meaning they listened and memorized. Even today, there is some controversy over this matter. Is it better to be formally and classically trained? Or, by learning by ear, can one develop a stronger, more vibrant musical tradition of one's own? The debate continues.

This was, quite likely, the first time Aretha Franklin's name appeared in the press. This was the beginning of something extraordinary.

Singing the Blues

Aretha Franklin grew up with popular music and the word of God practically entwined: to her, there was little difference between the two. As long as she continued to sing for gospel audiences, she believed she was fulfilling a divine mandate. But she did feel another attraction calling her: the blues.

C. L.'s prominence in Detroit's African American community meant that the family was exposed to all sorts of important singers and composers. Diana Ross, later famous as lead singer of the Supremes, lived only a few streets away. Aretha was exposed to leading ladies of gospel

Like Franklin, Sam Cooke started out as a gospel singer who shifted to singing the blues.

singing at an early age. But from Aretha's own account, it was the appearance of male gospel singers, Sam Cooke especially, that brought a strong pull to a relatively new form of music:

> Some men can sing, charm, and shine; some are easy with their good looks, others radiate confidence. Sam had all of this and more—the personality of a prince and a voice to match. He was one in a million.[4]

When Aretha Franklin first met Sam Cooke, he was the biggest male star in gospel singing. But Cooke soon transitioned to the blues and made far more money, as well as earning ever-increasing fame. While this caused serious consternation in Cooke's church, to Aretha, watching from the sidelines, Cooke made just the right move.

In early 1960, Aretha Franklin announced to her father that she wanted to pursue a career as a singer of the blues. Many people believed this decision was a mistake. Some believed it was sinful, that Aretha should devote her god-given talent to singing God's word. But C. L. Franklin made his feelings crystal clear in an interview with a leading African American newspaper:

> I am not one of those ministers who frown upon popular or jazz music. I believe that good Christian people can be involved in the popular field. Some of the finest stars in that field are among my respected personal friends. What would the world be without music and without a diversity of types of music? Aretha may have left the gospel field. But she has not left the church nor turned her back on the religious training she received.[5]

Just to ensure he was perfectly understood, C. L. declared that "Aretha is switching to the popular field with my permission."[6]

With the full support of her father, Aretha left her home in Detroit in January of 1960. Her first address was the YMCA on East 38th Street in New York City. And while this beginning may seem humble, Aretha Franklin was about to take the world by storm.

The Rough Side of the Mountain

The year 1960 was one of great change for Aretha Franklin. She left her beloved Detroit, exchanging the Motor City for the Big Apple. She was quickly signed to a recording contract. But she was also separated from her two children.

Mysterious Men

Even today, with decades of retrospect, very little is known about the men in Aretha Franklin's early life. What is quite certain is that she was pregnant at the age of twelve and again at fourteen.

> Was I innocent? Naïve? Vulnerable? Lovestruck? Yes, all of the above. I was a red-blooded African-American teenage girl, in love with love and the dance of love...But let me make this clear—I was not boy crazy, and I was definitely a one-man young woman. You had to be extremely special to get my attention.[1]

By the early 1960s, Aretha Franklin was recording with Columbia Records.

Aretha Franklin named her first child Clarence, after her own father. Given the absence of their fathers, the babies quickly became the loves of her life. But she could not take the children with her to New York City. Franklin left her young sons in the care of her grandmother, whom everyone called "Big Mamma."

The First Taste

Franklin arrived in Manhattan to face all the normal perils and pitfalls of life in a new, exciting, and occasionally dangerous city. She could easily have fallen into any number of predicaments that pulled her away from her singing career. One thing she possessed, however, was the same strength and perseverance that her father had as he moved from the Delta to Memphis, and from Memphis to Buffalo, and finally from Buffalo to Detroit. In each situation, her father had found his feet. So, too, would Aretha Franklin. Thanks to the Franklin family, Aretha also had a number of connections to draw upon. Within weeks of arriving in Manhattan, she was singing in Greenwich Village, and within months she had an audition with a major talent scout.

John Henry Hammond was one of the outstanding talent scouts of the twentieth century. Born in New York City and raised as a child of white privilege—including descent from the Vanderbilt family—Hammond became a discoverer of talent. He was the first to grant an audition to Billie Holiday, and he was one of the first to listen to Aretha Franklin sometime in 1960. Captivated by the strength and range of Franklin's voice, Hammond urged Columbia Records to sign her to a recording contract. The six-year

John Henry Hammond launched the careers of numerous legends, including both Aretha Franklin and Billie Holiday.

term included 5 percent royalties, no small feat for a brand-new talent.

The First Single

Aretha Franklin began recording right away. In 1960, at age eighteen, her first single came out. Entitled "Today I Sing the Blues," it became the signature song of her early career. She sings mournfully of a love gone wrong—one lost suddenly after the thrill, excitement, and fulfillment of just a short while before. The lyrics were not Franklin's; they were written by Curley Hammer and Curtis Lewis.

The sentiment was anything but unusual. Millions of women—white and black, rich and poor—could have said much the same. But there was something truly special in the way Franklin delivered the lines, accompanying herself on the piano. A star was born when the single came out.

A Star Finds Love

While her career took off, Aretha Franklin's love life continued to be complicated. She had an incredible knack for choosing the wrong sort of men, drawn to those that would take advantage of her. But things seemed to improve when she met, and quickly married, Ted White.

A musical promoter in Detroit, Ted White appeared to be a good match for Franklin. Both possessed quick minds and plenty of passion. But while they shared drive, determination, and a love of music, their relationship was

American Music in 1960

The 1960s had only just begun, but one could already detect a change in popular music. The Big Band era, which flourished in the 1930s and 1940s, was over and done. A handful of leading singers—Frank Sinatra in the lead—dominated the popular music scene. But when young people listened for new voices, they heard few African Americans. The blues scene was dominated by singers who had risen in the 1940s and were not ready to yield their place at the front.

Ted White, Franklin's husband and manager (center, pictured with Atlantic Records' Jerry Wexler and Franklin) was reportedly controlling and abusive.

rumored to be abusive. Franklin was just nineteen when she married Ted White and, perhaps owing to her young age, her husband began to dominate almost every aspect of her life. As her manager, he dictated what kind of music she should sing; as her husband, he hurt her severely enough to leave visible bruises.

Even with the stress of a volatile marriage, Aretha Franklin continued to sing and perform, working hard to build her career. Meanwhile, the record company continued to call.

Swingin' Singer

In March 1964, *Ebony* magazine ran its first photographic profile of Franklin. Entitled "The Swingin' Aretha," the essay had a photograph of Franklin on a swing set in a public park, relishing her new position as a force in the world of music. Franklin's background and her evolution as an artist were of particular interest to *Ebony*:

> Of all the singers who have forsaken church choir stalls for smoky dens of jazz…few have managed to fuse more "pure Gospel" into their blues preachments than a 21-year-old, Memphis-born, former singing evangelist: Aretha Franklin.[2]

By sheer coincidence, the same issue of *Ebony* profiled the sudden, shocking death of the singer Dinah Washington, whom Aretha Franklin much admired. No one planned it, but Washington's death created a void that Franklin was destined to fill. As *Ebony* asserted, Franklin seemed headed in only one direction, "to the top of the success ladder."[3]

Acknowledging a Debt

African American musicians began making it big during the early 1960s. One reason for the change is that leading white performers–including Elvis Presley, the Beatles, and the Rolling Stones–finally admitted their debt to earlier black musicians. Presley in particular was a lightning rod for criticism of appropriation and exploitation of a musical style that had been pioneered by black musical artists. On some level, it appears that Presley himself agreed: "A lot of people seem to think I started this business. But rock 'n' roll was here a long time before I came along. Nobody can sing that kind of music like coloured [sic] people. Let's face it: I can't sing like Fats Domino can. I know that."[4]

As black musicians began to receive more credit for their contributions, several black all-female groups, including the Supremes, were on their way to the top. This, in turn, set the stage for solo artists like Aretha Franklin to burst onto the scene–and impress everyone with her powerhouse talent.

The *Ebony* profile made much of Franklin's natural-born talent but also declared her a hard worker. Not many young singers could accompany themselves on the piano, and few put in so many hours of rehearsal. Even though there were rumors that all was not well in Franklin's marriage, *Ebony* gave generous coverage and attention, to Ted White who "is guiding [the] singer's career in transition from teenage singer to sophisticated adult artist."[5] But the most poignant words came from Aretha Franklin herself. When asked how she had weathered the tough years of her career, she responded, "It's the rough side of the mountain that's easiest to climb; the smooth side doesn't have anything for you to hang on to."[6]

The photos from the *Ebony* feature showed Franklin at ease, with her family, her newly arrived son, Ted Jr., at the piano, and practicing her golf swing from the privacy of her Detroit apartment. Most *Ebony* readers envisioned a smooth life for the young singer, but her skill at singing the blues indicated otherwise: she had enough experience with suffering to sing as well as she did.

Personal pain was one thing. Race-based pain was another. And in this area, too, Aretha Franklin was about to take a prominent place.

Love Songs and Civil Rights Marches

By 1964, Aretha Franklin already had more success than the average person—black or white—could ever believe was possible. She was continuing to record for Columbia, and she now had three children at home. But Franklin's personal struggles were about to merge with those of the African American community.

Taking a Stand

The civil rights movement had its strong beginning in the Deep South. Led by Reverend Martin Luther King Jr., Reverend James Abernathy, and others, African Americans made major progress during the early 1960s. The Montgomery Bus Boycott had already ended in success in the previous decade, and several other cities, including the metropolis of Atlanta, were integrated with much less struggle. But the same could not be said of the northern cities.

Aretha Franklin's star began to rise throughout the 1960s, a testament to her natural talent and her hard work.

In the summer of 1963, Martin Luther King Jr. was focused on the March on Washington, where he would deliver his "I Have a Dream" speech, the most famous of his career. But in the spring of 1963, Reverend King was invited by Detroit's African American community to visit the Motor City. Given that nearly all his success had been in the Deep South, King was eager to test his voice—and that of the civil rights movement—in the North. He, therefore, came to Detroit in June 1963.

C. L. Franklin was one of more than a dozen ministers who arranged the event, but to the photographers—and millions who viewed the photographs—it seemed as if Reverend Franklin was in charge and that he was number two only to Reverend King. Photographs show a beaming C. L. Franklin and a more somber Reverend King marching together in the streets of Detroit. This was the public face of the event. But a more private face was shown by another photograph, one that shows Aretha Franklin with Dr. King. Historian David Maraniss describes the encounter thus:

> Reverend Franklin, who already had occasioned a miracle of sorts with the successful and peaceful march, accomplished something equally extraordinary now, sublimating his ego by serving as emcee rather than main attraction. There were those who had heard both who thought Franklin could outperform King onstage or at the pulpit, but the pitch of his hum now was limited to brief remarks interspersed among more than twenty speakers.[1]

This meeting of talents was an outstanding moment for C. L. and the entire Franklin family. They played a big role in bringing King to Detroit. King delivered, giving one of the speeches that anticipated his amazing success in Washington, DC.

The significance of this monumental event was likely not lost on Aretha Franklin. According to the Rev. Jesse Jackson, who accompanied Dr. King to numerous civil rights marches, Franklin was a staunch supporter of black activism: "She went on a 11-city tour with Harry Belafonte and gave all the money to Dr. King," apparently saving the movement from certain bankruptcy.[2]

Crossing to Atlantic

Even as Aretha Franklin was involved in the struggle for civil rights, her career continued to grow. Though she was favorably profiled in *Ebony* in 1964, the next two years were disappointing as record sales were concerned. In 1966, Franklin contemplated a move to Atlantic Records. Jerry Wexler was the go-between person who eased the transition and paved the way for Franklin's biggest set of hits.

Born in the Bronx, Wexler was a scrappy entrepreneur who knew a good thing when he saw one. Wexler recognized Franklin's talent immediately and lured her from Columbia Records to Atlantic. Once Franklin was safely aboard, Wexler developed the idea of giving her a new backup band, composed of white southern musicians from Alabama. Aretha Franklin showed no nervousness over parting with her former group, and she soon hit it off with the new fellows.

The rest, as they say, is history.

Released in 1967, *I Never Loved a Man The Way I Love You* was Aretha Franklin's breakthrough album.

Crafting a Legendary Record

Franklin recorded *I Never Loved a Man the Way I Love You* in the winter of 1967. She and her band had a quiet confidence about the album, but they had no way of knowing just how far it would go.

I Never Loved a Man was released to radio stations on March 10, 1967, just two weeks before Franklin's twenty-fifth birthday. The singles were released one by one, and the record stores announced near pandemonium as Americans rushed to get their hands on the new vinyl. What was it about *I Never Loved a Man?* What brought the consumers out by the tens, and then hundreds of thousands?

The sound of Franklin's voice was surely the number one reason. The fine instrumental backup was a second. But the timing was also important. In the spring of 1967, Americans had much to be disillusioned about. The war in far-off Vietnam was going badly; the promises of President John F. Kennedy's New Frontier were largely unrealized; and real equality between blacks and whites, men and women, seemed about as far off as ever. Very likely, Aretha Franklin did not expect, or predict, the massive response. But it was there, almost from the first day that the album was played on the radio.

Hit Single After Hit Single

"Respect" may have sold the most, but four other singles from *I Never Loved a Man* were close behind. "Drown in My Own Tears," the title track "I Never Loved a Man," and "Soul Serenade" were all well liked, but these songs were written by other artists (Henry Glover, Ronnie Shannon, and King Curtis and Luther Dixon, respectively). In a bittersweet twist, it seems that fans were most enthusiastic for Franklin's songs, especially "Dr. Feelgood," cowritten with her husband, Ted White.

A New Level of Success

In the winter of 1968, American musical icons gathered to decide on the big winners of 1967. The Rolling Stones and the Who led the pack, but Aretha's *I Never Loved a Man* was the outstanding success from a native-born American artist. The popular reception was such that the Grammy Award leaders created a new category: best rhythm and blues album, and the honors went to Aretha Franklin.[3]

Could one person receive this much adulation? Franklin seemed completely up to the challenge. When the mayor of Detroit, Jerome Patrick Kavanaugh, declared that February

AM vs. FM Radio

AM radio came first and was in the lead, but FM radio was coming on strong. AM stations sent out an enormous blast, which could carry the sound long distances, while FM concentrated on delivering a crystal-clear sound in a limited region. AM and FM radio listeners were frequently at odds, but on one thing they agreed: Aretha Franklin's new album was the best thing around.

Franklin was a strong supporter of Dr. Martin Luther King Jr. and his civil rights advocacy for many years.

16, 1968, was Aretha Franklin Day, Franklin was on hand to receive all the compliments. And, by a rare chance, she was photographed with Dr. Martin Luther King.

Franklin's hair was styled in the de rigueur bouffant style of the 1960s era, and she sported cat-eye makeup as she clutched a plaque commemorating the occasion. King stood beside her, smiling, seemingly pleased to be present at what was essentially a publicity op for a beleaguered midwestern city and its favorite daughter. The reverend was in his customary dark suit, white shirt, and dark tie; what was unusual was the sense of casual joy projected by the man so often portrayed in photos and film as solemn, burdened by the weight of his work.[4] This was a happy, even ecstatic, moment for Aretha Franklin. But it was also the last time she saw Dr. Martin Luther King Jr. alive.

A Return to Gospel

In Memphis, Tennessee, on April 4, 1968, the Reverend Martin Luther King Jr. was assassinated.

It was a terrible year in American politics and society, with Robert F. Kennedy also falling to an assassin's bullet. African Americans felt both losses keenly, in part because Robert Kennedy had shown such interest in improving the lives of black Americans. But the death of Martin Luther King left many black citizens devastated and rudderless for some time.

The Passing of an Icon

Martin Luther King's funeral was held in Atlanta, Georgia. Though numerous writers have asserted Aretha Franklin sang at the event, this seems to be a legend that took hold after Aretha performed "Precious Lord, Take My Hand" at a Southern Christian Leadership Conference in August of 1968, where Martin Luther King Jr.'s widow, Coretta Scott King, and their children were in attendance. In truth, the Franklin family was as devastated as the majority of

While the end of the 1960s were a great time of personal struggle for Aretha Franklin, she still performed and recorded.

African Americans, and they were happy not to have to hold the spotlight at that difficult time.

For Aretha Franklin, King's death was a landmark. The optimistic spirit of her early adulthood was replaced by a fiery vigor, one that earned her trouble, as well as applause. The political scene in the wake of King's death was equally tumultuous. Franklin sang at the opening ceremony of the Democratic National Convention in Chicago that same year. This was not one of her standout performances— some claimed it was too loud, while others declared it lackluster. In either case, Franklin's role was soon forgotten, as the Democratic Convention lapsed into a scene of law-breaking, violence, and dissolute behavior. By the end of 1968, Aretha Franklin was still number one on the popular charts, but she also experienced disillusionment with her marriage and her career.

Walking Away

It may have taken some time to see, but Ted White was one of the great mistakes of Franklin's life. In retrospect, it makes perfect sense that she would desire such a powerful, embracing, but also conflicted man: he stood in for her father's positive and negative qualities. Deeply unhappy in the abusive marriage, the couple divorced in 1969 and broke off all contact. Franklin later said that they spoke about once a decade after the divorce.

A Return to Gospel

Though this may have been a difficult time for Franklin personally, she worked steadily through the late 1960s and early 1970s. In 1972, Franklin established close contact with Reverend James Cleveland. Raised in Detroit, he had been director of C. L. Franklin's choir at New Bethel Baptist Church while in his twenties. Cleveland had tutored the then eight-year-old Aretha on the piano, and she naturally gravitated to him, as one of the few older male figures she could trust.

Franklin was still with Atlantic Records, with Jerry Wexler as her guiding star. Wexler agreed that a venture into old-time gospel singing might do Franklin's career some good, and the two planned, with Reverend Cleveland, a major recording event at New Temple Missionary Baptist Church in greater Los Angeles. The recordings were made at a two-day session in January 1972. The album was called *Amazing Grace*.

Amazing Grace

Not one of the fourteen songs on the album came from Aretha Franklin as a songwriter or even from the gifted pen of Reverend Cleveland. All of the songs were gospel staples that the typical African American churchgoer had heard many times. But the music that was made, the definition stamped on the lyrics, was a brilliant combination of Franklin and Reverend Cleveland.

"Mary Don't You Weep" kicks off side A of the first record. The scene is Mary at the tomb of Jesus, but Franklin gives it special meaning and emphasis. Here is the son of God, risen from the dead: No one should weep, regardless of the pain they endure.

Martin Luther King Jr.'s favorite hymn, "Precious Lord, Take My Hand," is the second song on side A. The song

In 1972, Franklin won a Grammy for Best Rhythm and Blues Performance for "Bridge Over Troubled Water."

was first written and recorded by Reverend Thomas A. Dorsey in Chicago (Reverend Cleveland had his earliest training from Dorsey). This was an easy number for Franklin, who had performed it many times.

"How I Got Over" is the first song on the B side. Franklin was singing for the entire audience, but one also feels a special connection to her failed marriage to Ted White. This is followed by "What a Friend We Have in Jesus," and the final song of the B side, "Amazing Grace," stretched to a spellbinding ten minutes and forty-five seconds.

Only a rare listener could resist the pull of this breathtaking album set. "God Will Take Care of You" and "Wholly Holy" truly take the listener to the proverbial mountaintop.

An Unprecedented Response

Atlantic Records had big hopes for *Amazing Grace*, but the popular demand far exceeded its fondest hopes. Within a few months, the two-album set had sold more than a million copies, and in the next year it sold another million. This was Franklin's biggest success to date.

The African American press had surprisingly little to say about *Amazing Grace*. Perhaps this was because African American readers—and listeners—were well-accustomed to gospel success. The white, mainstream American press was more vocal in its praise, declaring *Amazing Grace* a sensation.

In the Wilderness

Up to the age of about thirty, Aretha Franklin seemed blessed with success. Despite a painful marriage and divorce, Franklin was the Queen of Soul and one of the highest-paid of all American entertainers, male or female. But then everything began to fall apart: love, family, and the recording contracts.

Wexler's Fading Presence

Jerry Wexler and Aretha Franklin were a fantastic one-two combination. Starting with the incredible success of *I Never Loved a Man* in 1967, they went from one hit to another, under the aegis of Atlantic Records. And when they brought out *Let Me in Your Life* in 1973, their style and presence seemed as solid as ever. Only two singles were released from the album, but one of them, "Until You Come Back to Me (That's What I'm Gonna Do)" won a host of awards and earned a great deal of money. In this song, Franklin takes on the role of a woman pining, waiting

Guided by Jerry Wexler, Aretha Franklin recorded *With Everything I Feel in Me* and *You* back-to-back in 1974 and 1975, respectively.

for a lover who, it seems, has abandoned her. The song was classic Aretha Franklin, even though the lyrics were written by Stevie Wonder. People were already calling the early 1970s the "Age of Aretha." But this tremendous success was the last she tasted in the 1970s.

Wexler and Franklin brought out *With Everything I Feel in Me* in 1974 and *You* in 1975. Both albums, particularly the latter, were major disappointments. What had happened? Franklin's voice was just as strong as in previous years. Jerry Wexler was just as adept at finding the right sound technicians. But the music went nowhere. The answer is that the popular music taste was changing yet again.

The Advent of Disco

Disco music is hard to define, but it had a strong emphasis on synthesizers and electronic keyboards and a powerful dance beat. While there were many talented singers in the disco genre, the music didn't require or showcase the kind of vocal power of someone

The popularity of disco music led to great success for singers and performers like Donna Summers.

like Aretha Franklin. Intended primarily as dancing music for young people at clubs called discotheques, disco music began to surge in popularity at the very time when Aretha Franklin's career began to wane.

Franklin was not the only soul or rhythm and blues performer to suffer from disco's rise. Other performers, including Diana Ross, had to change their vocal style and appearance. But Aretha Franklin suffered the most because she had the most to lose. As the Queen of Soul, she stood atop the popular music social pyramid, and as disco rose, her fortunes dropped.

Born in Boston in 1948, Donna Summer was six years Franklin's junior, but once the train of her success began to move, it was nearly unstoppable. In 1975, Summer shot to stardom with the single "Love to Love You Baby," and it was followed by "Last Dance," "Hot Stuff," and "On the Radio." For the first time, Aretha Franklin felt eclipsed by a fellow African American female vocalist.

One can, of course, suggest that rhythm and blues and disco were so different that there was enough room for two queens at the top. But the marketplace proved different. Enormous amounts of money, in advertising and record sales, fled the rhythm and blues market, headed in disco's direction. And even Jerry Wexler had no answer to the perplexing problem. In her autobiography, Aretha Franklin took a more positive view of the late 1970s:

> It really was a shame how many traditional R&B artists suffered in the disco days...My record sales slumped only slightly at one point, even though later I would return to gold and platinum.[1]

Disco's Peculiar Allure

Many critics have dumped cold water, or light praise, on disco. But the genre had to have had something appealing about its music, or else millions of young people would not have flocked in that direction. On examination, one finds that the music and the peculiar appeal of the discotheque, complete with strobe lights and pulsing sound, provide the answer. It was a social activity, the background noise for young men and women to meet each other in a nightclub, to dance, to have fun, and to connect, almost similar to how EDM–electronic dance music–functions in today's clubs. Disco was incredibly powerful, but its heyday was brief. The late 1970s represented the peak, and by about 1983, disco was seldom discussed.

A Second Marriage

Aretha Franklin had a brief romance with her road manager, Ken Cunningham, that resulted in a son, Kecalf. However, she wouldn't marry again until almost a full decade after the end of her first marriage. In an unusual twist, Franklin—already an icon in her own right—admired her future husband before they ever met. A native New Yorker who had relocated to Los Angeles, Glynn Turman had been working as an actor since he was thirteen years old. He appeared on the popular primetime soap *Peyton*

Place from 1964 to 1969 and was a successful, award-nominated theater actor to boot.

Backstage at a Ben Vereen performance, Clarence Franklin (Aretha's son) immediately cornered Turman. Clarence was eager to tell Turman that his mother "just loves you." Turman was all too happy to be introduced to this famous fan. Clad in a white dress and pearls, Aretha Franklin met her second husband for the first time. Both let out a little scream of surprise and admiration. They married in 1978.[2]

Glynn Turman and Aretha Franklin were much better suited than Franklin and Ted White, but there were complications from the start and sacrifices to be made. The couple settled in California, placing them far from Franklin's roots and family. Though the passion that brought the couple together was strong, it proved insufficient to carry them through rocky times. Turman brought three children to the marriage; Franklin had four sons; and the stepparents had to adjust their lifestyles to make room for the newly joined family. Even so, the marriage might have made it except for the family tragedy that struck in the summer of 1979.

Devastation in Detroit

On June 10, 1979, Aretha Franklin and the rest of her family were shocked to learn that C. L. Franklin had been attacked and assaulted in his Detroit home. The four men who broke into the home do not seem to have realized who C. L. Franklin was; they simply saw the house as a good mark. On entering, they were confronted by the elderly man, who had long kept a pistol close to his

Sibling Rivalries

That the Franklin children were close cannot be argued. That they went through all manner of highs and lows, ups and downs, is also beyond question. One aspect of their lives that frequently escapes the light of day is the intense rivalries between the siblings. Aretha was always the star of the family, but there were times when it seemed either her elder sister Erma, or her younger sister, Carolyn—both talented singers—might catch up. But though the Queen of Soul loved her siblings, she was truly peerless.

bedside. Whether he got off a shot or not, C. L. was soon overpowered and beaten. When Aretha and her siblings arrived, they found their father in a coma.

Of all the tragedies Aretha had experienced, this one—the attack on her father—wounded her the most. Ever since her mother's death, Aretha had been unshakably close with her father and saw him as the pillar of the family. Very likely, she swept under the rug many painful memories from her childhood, and she turned C. L. into a paragon of virtue. Now, as his primary caregiver, she had to confront the reality of his mixed legacy as well as her own role as the grieving daughter. "The emotional consequences were devastating for all of us," Aretha wrote. "Daddy was not only our father; since the death of our mom in 1952, he had also been our mother. He had been our everything."[3]

Aretha and her sister Carolyn (*left*) greatly admired their father, C.L. Franklin.

After this sudden, heartbreaking turn of events, Aretha moved back to Detroit. Her marriage suffered accordingly, and she and Glynn Turman separated in 1982, and ultimately divorced in 1984. When asked about the dissolution of her marriage, Aretha replied that her family, her father especially, meant the world to her and that she had no regrets.

Who's Zoomin' Who?

The summer of 1980 was neither an exciting nor an optimistic time. Americans were depressed over the longstanding Iran hostage crisis. They were not certain of the nation's direction. But, as sometimes happens in that time, a summer blockbuster movie came out, spreading feel-good laughter in all directions.

The film was *The Blues Brothers*. The subject—treated very lightly—is the introduction of the blues, as well as rhythm and blues into American pop culture. And one of the many show-stealers was a thirty-eight-year-old Aretha Franklin, who chose a particularly apt way to reintroduce her personal brand.

A Mission from God

Released by Universal City Studios in June 1980, *The Blues Brothers* ran two hours and twenty-seven minutes. The film opens with Jake (portrayed by John Belushi) being released from prison and picked up by his adopted

The Blues Brothers (1980) featured an extremely memorable cameo by Aretha Franklin.

brother Elwood (played by Dan Ackroyd). Raised in a Catholic orphanage, somewhere in the Midwest, the brothers revisit the orphanage, only to discover it owes back taxes and that it will soon be closed. This puts the brothers on a self-proclaimed "Mission from God," meaning they must reunite their former blues band and raise the money.

A series of scenes, ranging from mildly comical to truly hilarious, ensue. James Brown, a legend from the early days of rock and roll, appears as an ambitious gospel preacher who bears more than a passing resemblance to the Reverend C. L. Franklin. Ray Charles also makes a guest appearance, playing himself. But for many moviegoers, Aretha Franklin, who appeared for all of six minutes, stole the show.

Jake and Elwood—Belushi and Ackroyd—travel to the South Side of Chicago seeking to put their band back together. After a stirring street scene, which highlights some excellent soul music, the Blues Brothers find the Soul Food Café, owned by a middle-aged black woman, played by Aretha Franklin.

The brothers come to persuade Matt Murphy, played by the actor of the same name, to rejoin the band. Murphy, who is dressed in a T-shirt that emphasizes his muscular build, is more than happy to say "yes," but his wife, portrayed by Franklin, corrects him on the spot, by singing the lyrics to her hit song "Think."

The words on the page do not quite convey the excitement generated by Franklin's voice. Just to make sure the audience becomes fully involved, three African American women (played by Brenda Bryant Corbett, Margaret Branch, and Carolyn Franklin, Aretha's youngest sister) jump up from the café stools to dance in the middle of the room.

The words are sung with great feeling, but they fail. Matt Murphy takes off his chef's apron, places it behind the counter, and joins Jake and Elwood. Franklin shrugs, and when she sees her second-line prep cook pick up a saxophone, she says "go on, then," implying that her song is far from over.[1]

It is only a six-minute scene in a movie of 147 minutes. But it is deeply memorable, and it reintroduced Aretha Franklin to an audience hungry for her voice.

The New Label

Franklin had been with Columbia Records (1960–1966) and then with Atlantic (1967–1979) for most of her career. In 1979, she made a big move to Arista Records, and with

With the release of *Who's Zoomin' Who?*, the 1980s marked a popular resurgence for Aretha Franklin.

that, her career began to pick up steam once more, Arista released *Who's Zoomin' Who?* on July 9, 1985.

Much had changed since the summer of 1980. Americans were in a better, though perhaps not glorious, mood. And while *Who's Zoomin' Who?* employs some of the same imagery as *The Blues Brothers* (highways, fast cars), it does so in a more completely joyous manner.

The first song, on the A side, is "Freeway of Love." Coming in at five minutes and fifty-two seconds, "Freeway" is an average-length song. There was nothing average about the energy, or the response, however. As so often, Franklin mixes her metaphors to great effect. She sings of sex and lust but employs a "vision in white," evoking the sensuality of rhythm and blues while also echoing back to

A Talent for Improvisation

Though she cowrote around ten original songs in the course of her career, Aretha Franklin's great gift usually involved taking someone else's melody and doing improvisation upon it. In the impressive body of her work, which includes eighteen Grammy Awards, the vast majority of her songs are borrowed from other songwriters. Whether it was Carole King ("You Make Me Feel Like a Natural Woman"), Otis Redding ("Respect"), or Don Covay ("Chain of Fools"), the song's authorship never seemed to matter; Aretha Franklin made these songs her own.

her gospel roots. Any competent singer could perform these lyrics well enough. But coming from Aretha Franklin's lips and powered by her incredible voice, they were like magic. Singing of a pink Cadillac and a radio playing their song, Aretha had done it again; she delivered a song that knocked everyone's socks off. On the same A side was another song—the title track—which she cowrote.

The single for "Who's Zoomin' Who," a song with undeniable energy, hit number two on the R&B charts and number seven on the Billboard Top 100. If anyone doubted that the soulful hitmaker had returned and had done so with a new twist to her repertoire, their doubts were erased with the first song on the B side. Recorded with the Eurythmics, Franklin and the synthpop band showed the world that "Sisters Are Doin' It for Themselves"; the song, like "Respect," was an anthem of female empowerment, all about women who can "stand on their own two feet," without the help of a man. The song struck a chord with women all over the United States.

Aretha Franklin was back.

Chapter 9

The Queen in Winter

Aretha Franklin's popular music comeback seemed assured in 1985. The Queen of Soul had flirted with the blues and pop, and she now made another return to gospel. But before that triumphant resurgence, she first had to face one of the deepest losses of her life.

Saying Good-bye

C. L. Franklin died in July 1984. Five years and one month had passed since the assault in his Detroit home, and in all that time C. L. never regained consciousness. Not surprisingly, the Franklin family went through a period of mutual recrimination, as well as direct grieving.

"Aretha was his favorite," her sister-in-law declared. "You had to be blind not to see that…But here's the thing about Aretha. She takes her suffering—and God knows she was suffering that day—and turns it into anger. That's just her way."[1]

Regardless of who "started" the fracas, it is undeniable that there was one on the day of C. L.'s funeral. Family

Though she missed her own Hall of Fame induction, Franklin and Al Green were on hand for the opening of the Hall of Fame in Cleveland.

tensions that had long since been swept under the rug suddenly emerged, with painful repercussions all around. Aretha Franklin seemed the person best able to ride out the storm, but her close identification with her deceased father made this impossible.

Entering the Hall of Fame

In a sharp turn from the personal difficulties she had endured years prior, 1987 proved to be Franklin's best year in more than a decade. In January, the second induction ceremony was held for the Rock & Roll Hall of Fame—and Aretha Franklin was the first woman to be inducted.

Franklin's induction wasn't just historic in that she was the first woman to receive such a high honor, she also led the way for other black female musicians to be inducted. Of the other fifty-five female artists honored by the Rock and Roll Hall of Fame as of 2018, thirty-two have been black women, including legends like Gladys Knight and Etta James.

But even with this stunning validation of her accomplishments, Franklin wasn't content to rest on her laurels. She had new plans: she intended to return to her gospel roots.

One Faith

One Lord, One Faith, One Baptism is a double album that was recorded in July 1987. Though filled with songs, the album had only three solo vocals, all of them performed by Franklin. *Rolling Stone* made memorable commentary, declaring that *One Lord* was both "the sound of a woman at once reveling in the glory of her God-given talent and reflecting on a history of pain and uncertainty that earthly success couldn't salve."[2] Seldom has any one sentence so poignantly described Franklin's journey (and music).

"Walk in the Light," "Ave Maria," and "The Lord's Prayer" are the three single vocals, but Franklin's family and friends were perhaps most delighted when a family trio (Erma, Carolyn, and cousin Brenda) sang a song of their own. Only insiders knew that this was the last time the family would be complete.

More Losses

Carolyn Franklin died of breast cancer in April 1988. Just a few days earlier, she had earned her bachelor's degree, and it seems that she held on just long enough to celebrate that triumph. Hers had not been an easy life. Records are patchy, but it seems she was estranged from her father for many years because she was openly gay. And no sooner did the Franklins go through this loss than they endured another.

Aretha Franklin's brother Reverend Cecil Franklin died one year after Carolyn. Erma and Vaughn Franklin survived for the time, but the family was dramatically reduced in number. And at about the same time, Aretha Franklin's career began a downward spiral.

Facing Setbacks

As surefooted as Aretha Franklin's music was, she often floundered where publicity was concerned. This is evident in her one and only *Sixty Minutes* interview, taped and released in 1989.

Ed Bradley was a prominent African American television reporter; he had been the black presence on *Sixty Minutes* for years. He came to the interview with high hopes, believing he could dispel some of the misconceptions that had built over the decades. But Aretha Franklin practically stonewalled him. Bradley alluded to Franklin's difficulty expressing herself: "Whatever you learn from Aretha when you sit down and talk to her, you've got to watch her onstage if you really want to know what she thinks and feels and agonizes about."[3]

In the early 1990s, Franklin's voice seemed as powerful as ever. She performed at incoming president Bill Clinton's inauguration in 1993. In spite of this highly prestigious honor, Franklin was beginning to fall out of favor. Two decades earlier, the music world referred to it as the "Age of Aretha," but her combination of jazz, soul, and gospel was not in style. Nonetheless, there was no denying that she was an icon.

Divas Live

In 1998, Aretha Franklin reminded the world that she was truly the Queen of Soul. The music network VH1 broadcasted a special called *Divas Live*, featuring several generations of legendary female musicians like Mariah Carey, Celine Dion, Carole King, Gloria Estefan, Shania Twain, and Aretha Franklin. Franklin led the other artists in a stunning rendition of "You Make Me Feel Like a Natural Woman," dominating the song with her impressive vocals. The other divas, while all enormously talented in their own right, could barely keep up.

Struggling to Move Forward

By the end of the 1990s, Aretha felt the need to reinvent herself. She cowrote her autobiography, *Aretha: From These Roots*, and spoke openly of her desire to attend the Juilliard Academy in Manhattan. Her enthusiasms came and went with amazing speed, however, and she entered the new millennium much the same as previous: an incredibly talented middle-aged singer struggling to find a new place.

Along with cowriter David Ritz, Aretha Franklin wrote her autobiography, *Aretha: From These Roots*, in 1999.

Aretha's older sister, Erma, died of cancer in 2002. The family cycle was nearly complete, and it was replete with tragedy and overly shortened lives. But there were losses outside the family circle as well.

Ray Charles had long been one of Franklin's strongest supporters. While admitting that she could occasionally behave like a diva, he continued to testify to her vocal skills, saying she was one in a million. When Charles died in June 2004, Franklin lost one of her best friends in the music industry. And when Luther Vandross died, in July 2005, she lost one of her best fellow singers, they had performed many duets together.

But Franklin was not yet finished. Disappointed with the major record companies, she chose to go out on her own. In 2006, Franklin announced the formation of Aretha Records. This brand-new, self-directed label was intended to get her over the many disappointments associated with Columbia, Atlantic, and Arista. But in spite of her high hopes, Franklin never ended up releasing any album under Aretha Records.

A Crowning Achievement

One final triumph remained. Aretha had sung at the inauguration of President Jimmy Carter in 1977 and that of Bill Clinton in 1993. Now she was asked to perform at the inauguration of Barack Obama, the first African American to be elected president of the United States.

Some questioned whether Aretha could pull off the fashion element of the performance. Her personal style had been scrutinized for years, wearing what critics would call poorly fitting and ill-suited clothing. But in January

Aretha Franklin's performance at Barack Obama's inauguration in 2009 was legendary because of her powerful voice—and her instantly iconic hat.

2009, Franklin rose to the occasion. Her clothing was, if possible, praised even more than her singing. Her gray hat was studded in Swarovski crystals and dominated by a giant, off-center bow—it became instantly iconic.

The inaugural singing was certainly beautiful. But, years later, when Franklin performed at the Kennedy Center honoring songwriter Carole King, President Obama was actually moved to tears. When a correspondent wrote, asking the reason for his emotion, the president replied as follows: "Nobody embodies more fully the connection between the African-American spiritual, the blues, R&B, rock and roll...American history wakes up when Aretha sings."[4] Though she had largely retired from public life as she struggled with health issues, her live performance—one of her last—of "You Make Me Feel Like a Natural Woman" illustrated that Franklin never truly lost her spark or her incredible talent. That spark would stay with her until the very end.

After a lengthy battle with pancreatic cancer, American legend Aretha Franklin died on August 16, 2018, at the age of seventy-six. Even while mourning the loss of the Queen of Soul, the world celebrated her decades of achievement and her invaluable contribution to music.

Aretha's Gift, Aretha's Legacy

$\mathbf{M}$any of those who study Aretha Franklin's life and career come away convinced she was one of the greatest singers of modern times. Even her sharpest critics acknowledge the sheer power of her voice, which boomed, crooned, or sighed its way through five decades in the public spotlight.

At the same time, there are many critics who assert Franklin could have achieved much more. What if she had stayed with the special mix of gospel and soul she pioneered in 1967? What if she had stayed with modern music and not made those occasional returns to gospel? None of the answers are simple. All of them reveal Aretha Franklin as a deeply complex person. But the sum total remains the same—she was a titan of the music industry.

Gospel with Aretha

As a teenager, Franklin was devoted to gospel music, and twice as an adult she returned to her roots. Tutored by her

At Harvard's 2014 commencement ceremony, Franklin was awarded an honorary doctor of arts degree.

father ("the man with the million-dollar voice") she had a flying head start on her competition. But even with the Franklin name, it seems unlikely she would have broken through to a mainstream audience without making the shift to soul.

Soul Through Aretha

Can soul music be defined? It is, surely, more a state of mind than a precise set of measurements. Aretha Franklin's great good fortune was to make the shift from gospel to soul at the time the general public was ready for something new. Prepped by Elvis, the Beatles, and the Rolling Stones (all of whom drew from black pioneers of rock and roll), white America was ready for a black voice. Had Otis Redding lived longer, he might well have been stiff competition, but his untimely death in 1967 opened the door for Franklin to become the undisputed Queen of Soul, with no visible rival.

Had Franklin's career come to an end in 1968, she would still be remembered as one of the great change artists of the 1960s. But she went on and on, thrilling fans and concertgoers.

Aretha as Pop Star

Having already become a mistress of gospel and the Queen of Soul, Franklin redefined herself one more time: as an aging pop star with plenty of clout.

Franklin's mid-career "moment" came in the *Blues Brothers* movie, which suggested she had many miles still left. She won almost half of her eighteen Grammy Awards after the age of forty. Her voice seemed just as strong in 1985 (*Who's Zoomin' Who?*) as it had in 1967 (*I Never Loved a Man*).

Right to the date of her last public performance in 2017, Aretha still had millions of fans for whom she was *the* voice: the voice of African American resistance, of black housewives, of white blue-collar workers, and of the 1960s. And that raises one more question: was she representative of the African American experience?

Aretha's Identity

Very likely, Franklin would define herself as black, female, and a singer, in that order. Thanks to her father's involvement with Martin Luther King Jr., she was very conscious of the civil rights struggle, which lasted long beyond the 1960s.

Her racial identification was primary but made even more poignant by her female status. Throughout life, Aretha Franklin identified with the downtrodden, black women most especially. When Angela Davis, a philosophy professor, radical feminist, and political activist, was jailed for a spurious connection to a murder case, Franklin would offer to pay Davis's bail. Franklin gave a passionate statement on Davis's arrest:

> Angela Davis must go free. Black people will be free. I've been locked up [for disturbing the peace in Detroit] and I know you got to disturb the peace when you can't get no peace...I have the money; I got it from Black people—they've made me financially able to have it—and I want to use it in ways that will help our people."[1]

When activist Angela Davis was arrested, Aretha Franklin offered to pay her bail.

Performing right until the end of her life, Aretha Franklin sang publicly for the last time at Elton John's AIDS Foundation gala in November 2017.

At her best, Franklin was unmistakably African American, singing of the struggles of her people. But her special talent allowed her to go beyond this, to be a figure who appealed to men and women, white collar and blue collar, upper and lower class, as well as black and white.

Aretha Franklin was a child of the 1950s, growing up at a time of roller skates and backyard barbecues. She became an adult in the 1960s and participated as fully as one can in the struggles of that time. Her magical moment was 1967–1968—a calendar year so exciting that it motivated her fan base for decades to come. At the apex of her career, for many decades afterward, and to this day, Aretha Franklin *was* the music.

Chronology

1915

C. L. Franklin is born in Sunflower County, Mississippi.

1929

Martin Luther King Jr. is born in Atlanta.

1936

C. L. Franklin marries Barbara Siggers.

1942

Aretha Franklin is born in Memphis.

1960

Aretha Franklin signs contract with Columbia Records.

1963

C. L. Franklin introduces Martin Luther King Jr. to Detroit.

1966

Aretha Franklin is lured away from Columbia and signs with Atlantic Records.

1967

She records *I Never Loved a Man*, one of the most popular albums of the 1960s.

1968

Aretha Franklin is named Queen of Detroit; she is celebrated by none other than Martin Luther King Jr.
King is assassinated in Memphis.
Aretha Franklin receives the unofficial title the "Queen of Soul."

1971

Aretha Franklin is profiled in *Ebony* magazine.

1972

She records *Amazing Grace*, a double studio album that proclaims her return to gospel.

1974

Franklin records her last successful album with Atlantic.

1975

Donna Summer emerges as the "Queen of Disco."

1977

Franklin sings at the inauguration of President Jimmy Carter.

1978

Franklin marries Glynn Turman and settles in California.

1979

C. L. Franklin goes into a coma after an attack in his home.

1980

The Blues Brothers movie is released, with a special cameo from Aretha Franklin.

1984

Reverend C. L. Franklin dies.

1985

Arista Records releases *Who's Zoomin' Who?*

1987

Aretha Franklin records *One Lord, One Faith, One Baptism.*

1988

Carolyn Franklin dies.

1989

Reverend Cecil Franklin dies.

1993

Aretha Franklin sings at Bill Clinton's presidential inauguration.

2002

Erma Franklin dies.

2009

Aretha Franklin sings at President Barack Obama's inauguration.

2016

Franklin receives fulsome praise from President Obama after a show-stopping performance at the Kennedy Center.

2017

Franklin performs for the last time ever at Elton John's AIDS Foundation gala.

2018

Aretha Franklin dies on August 16.

Chapter Notes

Chapter 1
Earning R-E-S-P-E-C-T

1. "'Respect' Wasn't a Feminist Anthem Until Aretha Franklin Made It One," National Public Radio, February 14, 2017, https://www.npr.org/2017/02/14/515183747/respect-wasnt-a-feminist-anthem-until-aretha-franklin-made-it-one.
2. Barbara O'Dair, ed., *Trouble Girls: The Rolling Stone Book of Women in Rock* (New York, NY: Random House, 1997), p. 93.
3. "Lady Soul: Singing It Like It Is," *Time*, June 28, 1968, p. 62.
4. Ibid.
5. "Lady Soul: Singing It Like It Is," *Time*, June 28, 1968, p. 63.

Chapter 2
Daughter of a Preacher Man

1. Aretha Franklin, with David Ritz, *Aretha: From These Roots* (New York, NY: Villard, 1999), p. 5.
2. Ibid.
3. Nick Salvatore, *Singing in a Strange Land: C. L. Franklin, the Black Church, and the Transformation of America* (New York, NY: Little Brown, 2005), pp. 61–62.
4. Salvatore, p. 123.

Chapter 3
Daddy's Girl

1. Aretha Franklin, with David Ritz, *Aretha: From These Roots* (New York, NY: Villard, 1999), p. 20.
2. Franklin and Ritz, p. 11.
3. "Capacity Audience Hears Rev. Franklin at Norfolk," *Norfolk Journal and Guide*, March 30, 1957, B11.

4. Franklin and Ritz, p. 50.
5. "Aretha, Known in Gospel Field, to Now Do Pops, Jazz," *Norfolk Journal and Guide*, February 27, 1960, p. 18.
6. Ibid.

Chapter 4

The Rough Side of the Mountain

1. Aretha Franklin, with David Ritz, *Aretha: From These Roots* (New York, NY: Villard, 1999), p. 57.
2. "The Swinging' Aretha: Revival Training Pushes Vocalist to Top," *Ebony*, March 27, 1964, p. 85.
3. Ibid.
4. Brian Ward, *Just My Soul Responding: Rhythm and Blues, Black Consciousness, and Race Relations* (Berkeley, CA: University of California Press, 1998), p. 136.
5. "The Swinging' Aretha: Revival Training Pushes Vocalist to Top," *Ebony*, March 27, 1964, p. 89.
6. Ibid.

Chapter 5

Love Songs and Civil Rights Marches

1. David Maraniss, *Once in a Great City: A Detroit Story* (New York, NY: Simon & Schuster, 2015), p. 178.
2. David Jesse, "Rev. Jesse Jackson Recalls Aretha Franklin Saving MLK from Bankruptcy in Church Service," *Detroit Free Press*, August 19, 2018.
3. Maraniss, pp. 182–183.
4. Matt Dobkin, *I Never Loved a Man They Way I Love You: Aretha Franklin, Respect, and the Making of a Soul Music Masterpiece* (New York, NY: St. Martin's Press, 2004), p. 5.

Chapter 7

In the Wilderness

1. Aretha Franklin, with David Ritz, *Aretha: From These Roots* (New York, NY: Villard, 1999), p. 161.

2. Melody Baetens, "Grapevine: Aretha's Ex-Husband Glynn Turman Talks About Their Romance," *Detroit News*, August 21, 2018.

3. Franklin and Ritz, p. 185.

Chapter 8
Who's Zoomin' Who?

1. *The Blues Brothers*, dir. John Landis, Universal Pictures, 1980.

Chapter 9
The Queen in Winter

1. David Ritz, *Respect: The Life of Aretha Franklin* (New York, NY: Little, Brown and Company, 2014), pp. 351–352.

2. Ritz., p. 373.

3. CBS News, "Aretha Franklin, the 60 Minutes Interview," https://www.cbsnews.com/news/aretha-franklin-the-60-minutes-interview/.

4. David Remnick, "Soul Survivor: The Revival and Hidden Treasure of Aretha Franklin," *New Yorker*, April 4, 2016, https://www.newyorker.com/magazine/2016/04/04/aretha-franklins-american-soul.

Chapter 10
Aretha's Gift, Aretha's Legacy

1. "Aretha Says She'll Go Angela's Bond if Permitted," *Jet*, December 3, 1970, p. 54.

Glossary

appropriation Taking something from a person or, usually, a culture for personal gain.

beleaguered Under great pressure or stress.

consternation Discomfort.

disco A type of music that emphasized synthesizers and electric pianos over vocals, often played at nightclubs known as discotheques.

gumption Drive and resourcefulness to pursue one's goals.

improvise Adding to something, usually a creative work, without planning it out beforehand.

inhospitable Unwelcoming.

March on Washington A civil rights march that took place on August 28, 1963, in Washington, DC, where Dr. Martin Luther King Jr.'s gave his famous "I Have a Dream" speech.

Montgomery Bus Boycott A protest conducted by civil rights groups where black men and women refused to ride buses because of the rules segregating black Americans at the back of the bus, while white Americans rode up front.

paragon A perfect model or ideal.

recrimination Blame or criticism.

sharecropper A farmer who lives on and tends to land owned by someone else and who must give the landowner a share of the crops grown.

soul music A style of music that became especially popular in the 1960s, combining influences from jazz, gospel, and rhythm and blues.

spurious Questionable.

Further Reading

BOOKS

Dobkin, Matt. *I Never Loved a Man They Way I Love You: Aretha Franklin, Respect, and the Making of a Soul Music Masterpiece.* New York, NY: St. Martin's Press, 2004.

Maraniss, David. *Once in a Great City: A Detroit Story.* New York, NY: Simon & Schuster, 2015.

Mayfield, Panny Flautt. *Live from the Mississippi Delta.* Jackson, MS: University Press of Mississippi, 2017.

Ritz, David. *Respect: The Life of Aretha Franklin.* New York, NY: Little, Brown and Company, 2014.

WEBSITES

Aretha Franklin | The Official Aretha Franklin Site
arethafranklin.net

The official website of Aretha Franklin.

Aretha Franklin: NPR
https://www.npr.org/artists/15662553/aretha-franklin

A collection of articles, videos, and interviews featuring Aretha Franklin

Aretha Franklin Brings President Obama to Tears Performing at Kennedy Center Honors
https://www.youtube.com/watch?v=8cF0tf35Mbo

A video of Aretha Franklin's moving Kennedy Center performance.

Index

**Charlotte
Etinde-Crompton**

**Samuel
Willard Crompton**

About the Authors

Charlotte Etinde-Crompton was born and raised in Zaire and came to Massachusetts at the age of twenty. Her artistic sensibility stems from her early exposure to the many talented artists of her family and tribe, which included master wood-carvers. Her interest in African American art has been an abiding passion since her arrival in the United States.

Samuel Willard Crompton is a tenth-generation New Englander who now lives in metropolitan Atlanta. For twenty-eight years, he was professor of history at Holyoke Community College. His early interest in the arts came from his wood-carver father and his oil-painter mother. Crompton is the author and editor of many books, including a number of nonfiction young adult titles with Enslow Publishing. This is his first collaboration with his wife.